What God Told Me To Do, Tell Them What You See

Climmer O Suder

CLIMMER O SUDER
PUBLISHING

What God Told Me To Do, Tell Them What You See

CLIMMER O SUDER

Chapter 1

T O TELL THEM WHAT YOU SEE was the direction I was given. In order for you to see or understand you have to see things through His eyes. This has always been the truth. Because any limitations you put are yours, God has no limitations. This really means that when you see or read something and say it can't be, it is that you have judged it unworthy. The fact is, if it is there, it is part of god's creation and plan. So rather than dismiss it you need to try and see all the things it can unlock for you. In thinking of God, you need to remember no name can contain him since when we name something we think we can define it. And as God told Moses you can't even conceive of all he is, so he said I AM. As an example of this, I would like to point out that Abraham's descendants included Jesus and Mohamed. So, these two religions of men were supposed to be supportive and trying to represent the same God, the God of Abraham. So, you see this division of our religions has led to the deaths of millions of people, even though the primary figure in both spoke of seeking the Father's will first, and not judging by man's standards. So, you see three of the main religions because each thought they were right, destroys others even though the same god created all. Like children fighting to be the parents' favorite, yet not realizing the parent loves them all and wants them to learn to do the things that will raise joy for all. This as usual came about because we did not listen to what they said but we listened to what others said about them and what they said. Today we say that people don't believe in God when in fact it

1

has come about because these religions fail to explain the truth of why things are or happen. This makes so much of their message untrue that people reject it as lies or mythology. In short, since it does not explain or correct it must be wrong. So, the reality is that they reject the God as your religion defines him not, that there is a god. It's just that you have told them so many things that are not factual, they cannot blindly accept something that is clearly, seemingly intentionally incorrect as real. Why would creation be required at all? What is the purpose of creation and why is all that is made here? We don't even explain why what they did is so significant in terms that can be so obvious that anyone could put two and two together and discover the answer clearly and plainly. We make things secretly that allows us to dictate to others what they should think or see. That is what men do because they are searching for meaning they can dictate and control instead of understanding the true value and the gifts that it contains. It is unfortunate but it is what is happening today and for some time now it is what I see of the world. There are other forms of religion, some at least do not resort to naming something they cannot describe, and yet know that joining it is what they should strive for. Some call it a state of being, or a mentally altered state. Then they kill themselves trying to find something that was within them all along, again a hard way to convince followers they really know what they are doing or where they are going. Hard to imagine that all are right but just seeing things from a limited perspective. These are the things I see around us today. I am blessed to know God as the only true father I have ever really known. Because I seek to know and understand him in everything, he has shown me more than I could even ask for. I will try to find the words to describe accurately what I saw and what I see now.

There are many ways that people are shown what Is truly your father. Sometimes because they insist that God must be apart from them, they don't even see, it as being a part of or separate from themselves they don't think of what they are aware of as being God. So, they do not see it as a form of God, they do not think that he is present in their life until some major event forces them to evaluate what has been. And even then, because of the choices they have made to allow things that dictate to them what is capable of generating their true value, some accept the things others say should make them happy or are the way that they must choose to find happiness. Not realizing when they do that, they have promoted something to the status of God in their life. That is why in many places in the scriptures you are urged not to seek or celebrate false Gods. If you put the whims and judgment of society above your own heart you open yourself to insecurity because only you can really know what you feel and why you feel that way. If that is what you have done you have made society your God, and it will never end well for you. Because you can never fulfill the desires of everyone. One of the other ways you can prop up false Gods is money. Money was man's way of approximating what your feelings are worth. It is never going to give you the joy real feelings will. Again, it is promoting society's attempt to replace God in your life.

So, you see there are many ways you can promote things to be as God in your life. Because all of them fail to be true you will usually end up feeling unfulfilled by these things. What God your Father gave you is the freedom to select whatever you will to be your guide. It is this freedom that is true because, by your own execution of this choice, you dictate what will provide comfort and true security in your life. While security may not be a physical thing it is real in the quality of your life. So, you need to select wisely when it comes to what grants true security. If you truly understand and have a good relationship with God, you need not fear no matter what.

You are energy and matter; your thoughts and emotions are energy. They are just as real as your physical being. Because of that, what you have chosen can either provide more energy or reduce your energy level. Just as food for your body, you need to find those things that will truly give more energy to your life. In order for that to happen you have to know and not doubt what you are doing will accomplish that. Since the energy of life is the gift that God gave you, through it he has begun to reveal himself to you. You cannot deny it without denying yourself. Like all things what is, does not have to prove itself to you. It is your choice how much you will be able to participate in. It is amazing how many people say they do not believe in God but seek to go to heaven. Just as your feelings are real but you cannot put them in physical view, which can be apparent even for those who say they don't believe. It is amazing we can see what we know exists yet deny some aspects of reality because we choose to. It is this ability that allows us to throw so much of the potential we have away. Because what is real does not require your judgment to exist, it is part of the plan and what will be reality. It is this understanding that I see and am trying to help others not only see but take control of.

I was told to tell them what you see. In order to do that you have to understand what I mean when I say I saw whatever I am telling you. If you think about it when you were learning your lessons, it was when it became clear to you, then it was what you saw. Many people say you cannot believe what you see today. They point to what they call the scientific method to prove the truth. And yet they do not realize that in every situation there are variables that can nullify the method. So, when I say I saw something it covered all the variables as well.

In this way, I can attempt to show you what has made me understand and know without doubt what is true and does not change. It is not a matter of judging anything, it is a method of allowing things to judge themselves and then using that knowledge to understand what I should do. It is seeing through another's eyes or perspective. It is as Jesus said, that he was in his father, and since he saw things through his father's eyes or perspective, his father was in him, and we are one. What he was saying was that his father's will was all that he was committed to. Not his own will but his father's, and since your will directs your energy, it is the father's direction of all energy that will be, in that end all will end in one. It is what he called all who would follow him to do. Not to judge but to allow each the freedom to judge themselves by what they said and did. because by our judgment traditionally we see Jesus' statement that his will was what the father must do, when in fact what Jesus was saying is that the father's will is all he wants to be. Men deified Jesus based on what they understood which is God was separate from them so they could not see themselves as part of God they could only accept

4

God as being a separate form, for this reason, any angel or heavenly visitor or messenger must always caution people who seek to deify them not to but God the father only. None of them seek to be worshipped but are repelled by it. The truth and the way and the light is to seek the Father's will only. and We fail to understand so much because we seek to be allowed to judge each other, again to be separate from, not one with God whose energies created and is in all things, when in fact because we cannot create feelings in others that refuse to give you the authority to allow your judgment to create feelings within them. We do not like this because feel we can remove the freedom that God gave them to choose. Rather than understand the only way to increase the value or joy those feelings can create is to share them with others capable of feeling the same things and enjoying them. I will attempt to tell you why I saw and knew what I saw and experienced was true. I can only tell you what I saw, not what you should choose, or that my understanding will change the quality of your life, that is up to you. By what you choose to allow illicit feelings within yourself. I can explain that whether you see it or not all that was needed to be, in order for creation to be, all that was required to allow it to complete the function it was created for, there is a corrective portion that is automatic and does not change regardless of your desire to control creation itself. As Jesus said we are one, but we are to perform the function the one, created us to perform. This first chapter is about the who, understanding that you are a child and therefore a part of the creator is understanding that the only true limits you have are self- imposed. I cannot describe all of the father; I can define how I relate and feel about him. However, understanding the purpose of creation and what it was designed to do. Helps to understand the totality of what it represents. Your definition is totally dependent on you. Understanding the rest of the story will help you to choose how much you will be capable of interacting. It also limits you to how and what you can do with the gifts you have. Your gifts and abilities are real. How you can use them is subject to the purpose of creation itself. So many people think that power is only relevant if you can use it how you choose. I will explain more about this later in this book, but if you understand and seek the will of the father which ultimately will be and should be the will of us all. It is truly this unity of desire that not only allows heaven but guarantees it will come.

Because you can see this progression you can see why things that were written a couple of thousand years ago, are not only true but inevitable. So, you can see prophecy in motion and understand why it must be and will be the truth. It may not work in the way that people have insisted it would, but the result will be. just as people say the fact that men killed Jesus even though he was innocent makes him the savior, the fact that people thought they could kill God and still he lived just as he said he would, so if you are as he was you can live as well. He was so certain of it that he told them what was going to be. Are you that certain of it as well? You need to be if you have faith in the size of a mustard seed. It is this faith without seeing that takes away the fear, you seek to be saved, but from what? Your fear, or your doubt. It sounds easy but I have seen and been to heaven and am part of our father, yet I had to understand there is an order to creation that serves his purpose. I am fortunate for I have seen and know; it is so much harder to believe without seeing. So, I was told to tell them what you see. So, if you will, just as you sought to see through Jesus' eyes, you will know the Father and no longer doubt and fear. It is this that I struggle to find the words to help you see. I also know that it will require the holy spirit's energy if you seek to experience this.

For you to know the father you must allow him to be, in whatever form or forms he chooses to help you see. By your decision to separate things and make them less than they could be you have difficulty accepting the creator of all. Because of this, you find yourself serving princes and principalities. These are the things you have given power to and in truth, they have no power over anyone who refuses to give them authority. I have not come to battle princes or principalities they are yours and only you can decide to be free from them. I serve the father and creator of all. I pay witness to what the son has told you because even if you don't know yourself you are a child of the father and while he gives you the freedom to do what you choose, he has put in order a system that will always support the truth. Your thoughts of being able to stop or change the truth by killing the messenger are to no avail. It is not the individual themselves it is the will of the Father to bless and increase those who seek to serve him and each other which is of him. The system, from the beginning, is done in a form that because it is not limited by your time or calendar will always have the desired results in spite of the fact that you only seem concerned with your physical time. In fact, because the energy that comes from God to give your life is your soul, and you are not only your body the manner in which you communicate with energy is different as well. As an example, I would ask you, have you ever done anything and knew instantly that it was going to cause you a problem? Or perhaps you have just met someone you knew was going to become significant in your life? There are senses that you have but rarely use because you cannot really explain how you knew or what you felt you thought people would think you were crazy or just foolish. For most people, these senses are probably used infrequently to become confident and secure of the source. I know there are people who because of what they're supposed to do are much more aware and accustomed to relying on those senses. As their history has proven to them that this feeling is true and learn, to not only listen to them but to become dependent on their feedback. in order to fully understand someone else's feelings, knowing how to listen to these feelings and trust them as well. Just as it is in your understanding of who or what God is to you, these understandings are as many as there are people. Your thoughts are yours for you to conduct life as you choose. Everyone has that right. If you feel the need to define God, you do not know him because he is more than you can conceive. So many people are so used to being separate from each other and even the energy of those around them such as pets or pack members, consequently they think of things in physical form and apart from themselves. However, they sense when they are being watched or someone is talking or thinking about them. This nonphysical you are still you and it is what binds us to pack etc. It is also how you are connected and part of the father and creator of all. Just as your DNA connects you to those who were before you. And because of that DNA, they are part of you. I tell you this so you understand you cannot think of God as a physical form apart from you. God is all forms of energy and everything he fashioned. The energy is contained even at a sub-cellular level at least one form of that energy, it is why the body becomes food.

For another, even vegetation cells become food. Even what we call inanimate objects contain energy we are just generally not aware of how to use it. This is important to understand since it is pivotal in the process and reason for creation and life itself. It is the purpose of the function creation was intended to do. This first chapter as I have said is about the who, I know that few experience the full impact of being one with the father because of their desire to be apart from, not part of. Once you experience that connectedness you can't forget it.

As I have said in my previous three books, I am writing about what I saw and experienced on my spiritual journey. This chapter is about the who, both you and God himself. God is all energies even types we do not know yet. My journey took me back through time to heaven before time.

While there I was able to be in the presence of God and experienced so much, that I can hardly find the words to explain, even a portion of the experience. But I know that this was created so we could have a portion of energy to exercise our will to raise or increase energy. This was so that we could share our father's will or set ourselves apart from our father. It is this increase we were created to be able to do. Energy always seeks to increase. As a result of this nature was formed to ensure that all things would be in order for increase to occur. In this manner independent of our will energy can seek to accomplish the Father's will always increase in spite of our desire to separate and therefore eliminate the capability of the energy of our feelings to weaken or remove energy. This is the second death that we can give ourselves, and the reason Jesus said we fear the one who can give us the first death but pay no attention to the one who can give us the second death. Since our Father is all energy with the will to direct it, we cannot define or limit him in a form because it would place limits on him. It is also why the energy begins and ends in him. He is the Alpha and the omega, the beginning and the end. Knowing now that we were given this portion to increase or remove our ability to participate in this growth. Each of us has received the portion of energy that we have to judge ourselves. To either increase the energy in the form of joy for ourselves and others or to separate according to our will which removes the ability to increase. God is always greater and continually greater. It is the purpose of creation to get greater, quantity and quality. It is our choice and will to allow what we would, to cause us feelings but if what we have allowed will not allow the increase nature itself can apply corrective measures. In this manner, creation itself will fulfill the purpose it was made for. All of these things were contained in what Jesus taught and explained in keeping with prophecies from long before him. It is this failure to understand he knew was going to happen and so he told his disciples in the end many will come to me saying lord, lord, and I will look at them and say, "Why do you call me lord, but you do not what I said?" I don't know you. You see it is understanding that God is the source of all energy, and we are here to serve him and allow that energy to do what it is formed to do increase. This message allows you to forgive and warns you never to judge what you do not know.

All of these things I saw and felt before time was and creation of this was done. This was the spiritual journey's beginning and if you consider it in detail you will see for yourself if you cannot, ask the Father and he will show you in his own way. But even though I have spent a life of interaction with him in ways I never paid enough attention to before this Journey, I knew him and was somewhat accustomed to him answering requests, yet in order to prepare me for what I was about to experience it took a brain injury that limited me severely and removed the typical response of that is not what society or the church teaches. That process of preparation took seven years and most of what I thought I had accomplished in life. So, I can caution you about what you ask for because many times the truth is not what you presupposed. This is just the beginning of what I saw and how it put all things in order and made them understandable, that is not to say likable. Things must be what they are and all things necessary must be therefore them to exist.

Chapter 2

I F YOU HAVE READ ANY OF my other books you know I am writing about a spiritual journey that I was taken on. This book in particular is my attempt to tell you what I saw and experienced on that journey and since that journey, it seems to have established an ongoing awareness of what I was shown. It is awful and overwhelming trying to find the words to describe what ultimately is indescribable. When I talk about what I saw I mean I felt it as well as seeing it. This is hard to explain but, becoming aware of senses that you have had limited use of suddenly becoming active is hard to explain. Because in our very dimensionally limited mind, we are accustomed to the very few dimensions we are used to because we are limited to the constraints of time and space. But experiencing this I did and was aware of being a part of not apart from the creator. It made me aware of being without the limit of time and even space so I could be in more than one place at once. This is the connection that the creator of all can allow you to feel. The first chapter was hoping to help you to seek your own relationship with as near a definition as I could find the words for, but invariably it is your own definition that comes from your understanding that you need to know. It is individually that we raise the Glory and value of all by sharing what we can with all. In other words, the first chapter was to help answer the WHO question. This chapter is hopefully to answer the WHAT question which is creation itself and how it serves its purpose and ordered all that was to follow. I hope you can see now that there is really no separation between you and the father other than those you empower.

As I was within the father, I was able to feel so much more that was there and had always been there I began to see the order and reason for all. Obviously, I was overwhelmed with this level of activity. It made me afraid to question him. Did not want to fail him, but I wanted to see all that he would show me. There was so much at once I had difficulty processing it. But this chapter is about creation itself. We like to think the creation was for us, however, the reality of creation requires that all that is needed for anything to be there, so a better explanation is that it was God's self-expression of what he is. Since all are in him it is the purpose of creation to complete who he is. This purpose provided the blueprint for all that would be. Everything must seek to get greater since he is always greater. This simple fact is the cause of all that is. It is because he is the beginning and the end always that removes the time-space continuum. Just as we struggle to improve ourselves through education and fitness programs including our diet so that we can function optimally in this dimension, so too in every dimension he is expressed as always greater. This is the purpose of the tree of knowledge of good and evil. Good always leads to more evil divides, it is always less than what could have and should have been. Because evil divides it allows us to define what we want differently, but because the purpose of creation is to always make more, unless what we do will accomplish this purpose, we will receive what is less than, therefore life itself is self-correcting and beyond our individual ability to change. It is for this reason that loving your brother as yourself is one of the cornerstones to accomplishing the purpose. When you do you not only demonstrate your love of them but of the father himself who we are all a part of and from. It is because of this you cannot give to someone something they cannot appreciate or know what its true value is, you have wasted that value and helped no one. This is the basis for the difference between sacrifice and mercy. Sacrifice always results in the loss of value, mercy always increases the value. Value is expressed in your joy and appreciation of life. There are so many ways that this can be made apparent and demonstrate how the failure to understand this has caused so much misery. Since sacrifice causes the loss of value and mercy increases value the results will either increase everything or cost individually. As an example, I have used the dead veterans of every conflict our nation has gone through. We say we honor them and appreciate their sacrifice, when in fact we do not value their freedom, they died trying to protect and provide for their families. That is why what they did is a sacrifice. However, if we feel as they did about our freedom we protect as they did that freedom and we do not elect officials who remove our freedom. I am not trying to be political I am being factual. It is the result of our choices that will either cause mercy or sacrifice to become apparent. It is this simple misunderstanding that has caused us to think of sacrifice as a good thing and not the constant loss of true value. I point out now what Jesus said to the Sanhedrin, "I do not require sacrifice, I require mercy, if you knew the difference you would know where my authority comes from."

Sacrifice is man's way of punishing people by removing their value, mercy is God's way of improving your value. I can only hope you will see this or go ask the father himself to show it to you. Unfortunately, so many will go to their church to answer this and just like the Sanhedrin, who were the leadership of the Jewish church they did not really know or understand the importance of this difference but knew the difference would remove their ability to demand sacrifice, and this would ultimately impact the economic structure of their world. The reason this is so vital is that you cannot have heaven here without knowing how true value is maintained. It is part of the learning process this time-space room was created for. So, you see this creation was not for you but the expression of our father to maintain the order of what his purpose is. There are many other ways that this understanding can be applied. We think of our room as the only room, but we reason that the chances of us being the only life forms in the universe seem practically impossible. But we discover new things all the time, for example, the universe itself is expanding at an amazing rate. Suppose that is for the purpose of keeping the rooms apart till the understanding of non-judgment will allow for the contact to be within keeping with the rise of value for all. There are other dividers than time space, but we can't seem to come to peace with these let alone nonphysical boundaries. All of this and much more became apparent to me as I became one with him. If you understand the purpose of creation was and is and always will be to expand and make God, however, you know him to become greater. Then you can see why whenever you divide or separate things you reduce their value, you can understand that it will always result in a loss if you do not serve the ultimate purpose of creation, this will always work the same and is the truth without regard to what you think or believe. You have the ability to affect how you the individual relate to the purpose of creation and you can seek to persuade others to allow you to tell them what they should think or believe or even what they are worth, and they might buy into it but it will not override the enforcement of the purpose of creation and it will usually result in the loss of life on an epic scale until despite your threats the individuals understand they are all the children of God the creator and they are meant to make things greater not to destroy their value or give it away. You see you are part of God not all of God. You are allowed to choose for yourself to serve all or limit yourself and how much of him you will share.

I know you want to know the nuts and bolts of creation, but you need to be able to understand that time is not applicable to God, so he used the energy that is him which is all energy. The different types of energy working with each other created the matter, and then they formed the DNA that allows a specific type of energy to form each individual being in keeping with the purpose of all to get greater. Just as it is even today solar energy works with thermal energy and pneumatic energy to form land masses as we know them. There are so many forms of energy just as within the individual there are so many systems to accomplish the growth of the individual.

Some of them we have yet to understand. We know there is matter and anti-matter, and we know many forms of energy and others we have yet to understand, we call this dark energy. All energy starts and ends in the creator. He is the beginning and the end; it is for his purpose all things do what they were designed to do. It is because we cannot put them into the time-space continuum we fail to see them even when is apparent the interaction since we cannot determine the time for the interaction. Consider the energy as the creators' fingers to form all things. We are only part of him, there is so much more than we can learn. Always keep in mind the purpose is always to create more if it is to accomplish this purpose. So, there are constant revisions to the DNA to allow changes in the individual to adapt and change to multiply in keeping with the purpose if this does not happen the extinction of that species will occur. This will become an important lesson in the form and place of where this creation is going. I will cover this in other sections of this book. Suffice it to say that the energy that is in and from God will do what it is to do in order for the purpose of creation to be fulfilled. We desperately want to understand and define all of these processes, but we cannot because we do not understand what it is like to be unfettered by time. I would hope you can understand now that time is only relevant to that which is contained by time located in a single space, that is only your body, not your energy which is the gift of life God gave you. It exists to fulfill the purpose of creation. It is your soul and your knowledge it is the remainder of how you have judged yourself by what you have chosen to allow to determine how you will feel about anything.

I have shown you that the purpose of creation is the increase of all things which are and in God, things get greater because he is always greater. I hope you can now see that in order to limit something that is without limit a new way of being was required. In order for that to occur a new form was required that could limit enough of that energy in a form that could still accomplish the purpose but allow the increase of the energy, which is the increase reflective of all that is the father. That required the formation of different guidelines we call natural instinct. This is for the continuation of the form which is contained in time yet allowing the increase or the decrease of the energy which is outside the form and therefore not subject to time. In this manner, each individual could work for the increase of the joy that is created by the joyful feelings created when shared. Because that feeling is so wonderful, we know it is good. It is the completion of the purpose of creation to make it greater. The opposite is also now available which is to reduce the joy by not being able to participate in it because of the things the individual chose to determine what and how much they would feel about anything. This duality of purpose creates many internal conflicts for the individual. You have a natural instinct to procreate in order for the species' form to be maintained. But it becomes one of the most basic and specific areas where men could exercise what they feel is power because they can dictate what they think you should be capable of feeling and enjoying. This is an example of how man seeks to replace what God has ordered. It is the loss of the value of procreation. It is one of the ways people try to say it because you experience these feelings you are obviously not worthy. In fact, the instinct came from God to always make more and greater. But your feelings are a combination of what you chose so if you understood that the joyous feelings are because you shared with the intent of raising the joy of life by sharing it with someone who feels like you. It is this horrible misunderstanding of the fact you were given the choice for you only, so by disregarding this you think you can have power over others which would make this seem untrue. It is this total misunderstanding that can result in sexually motivated crimes, especially in war because the whole order of things is a question for the participants. It is horrible but it also points out what mercy or holding the individual accountable for how they judged themselves by what they said and did. If they seek to harm others, they must be harmed. If you do not honor their judgment of themselves, you enforce their decision as an acceptable course of action, and by rewarding it you create more. This failure is due to the notion that sacrifice is good. It does not serve those who seek to do the correct things in increasing the joy for all. Your judgment of another will always result in the loss of true value. Holding them accountable for what they did is justice. It was the basis for true justice. Not guesswork but beyond a reasonable doubt that it is what they did. Attorneys collect funds to try to mask the reality of what happened, if they do what they should they do not represent someone they know the proof is without a doubt that they did it. Again, some value money so much that they will do anything to shield their client. Again, this is removing the consequences of what they did, it allows them to not learn. You think that it is God's will that people should be given all the chances available to them. In reality, God uses their feelings to punish and make their lives miserable so all you have done by removing the punishment is prolong their misery which will generally end up in the suffering of someone who is caught up by chance. I have used this clearly criminal example to demonstrate the extreme that is possible as a result of sacrifice. It is also apparent in the political process of men. I am suggesting that you understand what you support as a sacrifice you think is good or entitled you will ultimately empower the loss of value in your society. Vote with the understanding that we are all here to raise the value of life which cannot be done if you insist on division or judgement of others. It is this that is going to end if heaven is to exist here on earth. You are choosing for only yourself will you be able to be in heaven? You think this is so unrealistic. But didn't the scriptures tell you that the Messiah would come and what would happen to him? You wait for him to return when his words and meaning have always been here. The things I talk about are his words. I am not saying what he did not, I am showing you the things I saw and were shown what you do with them is how you judge yourself. Consider that in the time of Jesus people expected God to do things the way they thought, the Messiah would come from a house of kings. It was his words and promises of our relationship with the Father that he demonstrated and called you to be as he is. One with the father. Understanding him and his will and striving to do those things which will make that real here. Let me ask you now, what are you looking for? An army to appear in the clouds forcing people to do what they say, why would you think that when it is so far from the way the father has dealt with us in the past? Did you hear what the prophets said, and that Jesus said mercy which is allowing each the freedom to judge themselves truly?

Allowing each to accomplish the function of creation which is to make greater? Or are you committed to judging others and condemning what the father made? In order for something to be all the things that define it also have to be, it is the individual's choice what portion they choose for themselves. So, do you support the loss of some, or do you just refuse to do what you know will cause harm to others? That is how heaven is, no one does what is not in keeping with the fathers demonstrated will. Granting each other the freedom God gave them to judge themselves, not supporting those who seek to divide or separate. Allowing those who seek harm to be harmed themselves because that is what they seek. This is what will be here as promised but you can see it does not exist with sacrifice. Evil and division will always be present because they define good. Just as the tree of the knowledge of good and evil was in heaven as well as in Eden. The question has always been what do you choose?

So, I hope you can see now maybe more capable of seeing why there was a requirement for this creation. It is an isolated place for you to learn and judge yourself and still accomplish the function that is required in this place. The fact it exists is without question, the purpose of it is something that you need to understand in order for it to perform its function in your life. I will cover this more carefully in the chapters to come.

Chapter 3

THIS CHAPTER IS ABOUT THE **WHEN.** It will be an exercise in how open to the father you can be. The question of when again is a matter of perspective. It is important to understand that when I say I want to talk to you, it is not that I don't want to talk to groups but that it does not matter what others hear, it matters what the individual feels as a result of the conversation. because each person was given the freedom by our Father to determine for themselves their world, this is the dominion he gave men, your world's value is established by your feelings, and is not to be subject to what others think or say. if you decide to allow their thoughts or feelings to replace yours you have given the dominion God gave you to them. As I said I have travelled back through time to experience and see what I am talking to you about. So, I can tell you that When is now. It is important to understand that this time is your portion to judge yourself. In order for that to occur you must have the freedom to choose what you will give authority over yourself.

That way you cannot blame others for what you chose. that is required in order to have Justice. The point of this creation is that you choose to increase the value or joy of the gift of life you have been given. If you raise the joy of life for yourself as well as for those who are in contact with you, you are accomplishing what God wanted for you. You are not responsible for what they choose but you must not seek to harm them. So, you see that even though we think in terms of lineal time you still get to choose what is for you. The problem comes when you think you have the authority to choose for others what they should choose. From what I saw I can guarantee that what has been foretold will happen. Heaven can and will exist here on earth the question is will you be able to participate in it? or will you set yourself apart from it? I have written three books about the place Jesus himself prepared for you while he was here and confirmed it by his resurrection which also is what he promised, I go I will return to show you there. In that, Jesus knew and still went through the crucifixion without fear and cursing others, he had the peace to overcome the fear even of death. in his words and understanding you too can access this place for yourself. Again, doing what he said and showed you. although most people would say it is impossible. It is another example of how he understood what was going to happen before it did. Which is that there was something beyond the physical that exists. Therefore, there are regions that exist that are not tied and directly connected to time. this understanding of an alternative reality is one of the gifts God has for us. Having experienced this I can attest to what I saw. As you can see from the question of when a matter is truly of the individual, I know that others point to time as they know it, what I can tell you is that there is so much more than what we currently know or understand. Consequently, your when is yours, however, there are things that were foretold that can help you to see where in history you are. I am going to tell you what I saw, what you do with it is up to you not your neighbor or your church or any social group.

There are always those who think their understanding is the only real appropriate understanding. I would remind you that before Jesus the people were told about the coming of a messiah, and they thought it would come from the house of kings. Also, you were told that in the end times, life would be pretty much as usual with people giving themselves up on marriage, etc. Do you think that would be the same if people saw an army in the clouds? or a figure they assumed was Jesus in the clouds? or do you think as before it could not be till they are revealed by what they said and did? Do you think such a major event would be hidden? although that is what most of the Christian churches tell you will happen. I would think that with today's media, there would be such a major uproar that the world would be informed. They were thousands of years ago. But as usual, people tend to look to others to tell them what they should believe. then they will accept what they think will give them popular approval. Unfortunately, I can promise you that if you judge anything other than yourself you will never be allowed in heaven, even on earth. What that means is the place that was prepared for you is not subject to others' judgment as well. It is a place that is inside the individual and not subject to others' judgment. If you give them the authority to tell you what you should believe or feel you will not participate in heaven as well.

This is the rapture that was talked about. we like to think we are physically removed but in fact just as Jesus disappeared for three days mentally and emotionally you can choose to be absent from the judgment of others. This isolation will be rapture because their judgment will mean nothing to you. Those who are wrapped up in judgment will destroy themselves trying to force others to accept their judgment. This includes the church just as it did in Jesus' time. however, this time the choice will be on an individual personal level that will remove the power they try to exercise over others.

As I went back through time, I saw snippets of the atrocity's men perpetrated upon each other and themselves in hopes of satisfying others' judgment. each horrible yet historically correct. all because they submitted themselves to the judgment and will of others. What do you believe and why? The trip showed atrocities and the reason that people subjected themselves to them. most of the time it is because they sought the approval of others rather than what is best for all. Many times, their precious items such as their children or relatives were given to support the judgment or greed of others. when man came up with the concept of money, they sought to have society tell you what you should feel value or want. as long as they can put themselves in the place that God created which was to give them the freedom to Judge themselves, they seek to nullify God's judgment. They always seek to find ways to get around judgment and to be able to say what will be. It continues today there is a war in Ukraine that is killing thousands because it is the will of a few people to take from other people. and the people of the nations of the world are allowing it. the people of the nations involved are giving their precious treasures such as their children and relatives. If you are doing this to take from others, you are violating all. If you are defending, you are defending for all. it is as it has to be since socialism seeks to remove God

19

who really is the source of freedom so they can decide who gets whatever value is in question. in this case, the people of Russia give their children to die in support of a political party's greed. in the United States, people give their money and treasure to another country in hopes of preventing the loss of their children. as it is in the rest of the world. what should have happened not because anyone wants it to, but because it is necessary to stop nations from violating other nations and the children of God once they have done this once, they will continue to steal from other nations. So, it is the judgment of the entire world how they have judged themselves worthy of destruction. I am not here for the politics or the approval of anyone except our father. so, the people of Russia deserve what is happening to their brethren the people of the rest of the world deserve to inherit the evil that they are allowing. the reason socialism has always been the abomination that causes desolation is that it does not support increase but takes from others and never produces enough to raise the Joy of All. Unless it has a victim, it cannot support itself. I am pointing out that it cannot exist with freedom even the freedom of God to exist. it must prevent everything even the Church from surviving. I have seen this ongoing atrocity and as long as the children give their support and votes to empower these atrocities they will continue. So, the United States by electing socialists threw away the freedom that God wanted for them and so many of their children fought to provide. So, anyone, or political figure that demonstrates themselves as socialist is an abomination to men and the will of God, if you allow this you deserve the atrocities, they will bring to you just as the people of Russia deserve the death of so many of their children and relatives. To the people of Ukraine, I can tell them to seek the Father and know that no matter what the world fails to do to stop this evil, God is who they will answer to. Just as the freedom to be is yours unless you give it away. If you believe in the creator do not give up what he has given you. To the rest of the world, you have cursed yourself by repeatedly allowing this and many atrocities. I know you think that it is the nation's or someone else's problem, but your nation uses your wealth and children to enforce their greed. How many are your children, fathers, brothers? uncles, grandfathers, or mothers' worth to you. your power is allowing these atrocities. I know the loss of any is horrible but if the world stood together and let the nations know that they are no matter how big or little they are they violate God's law by invading their neighbor must be destroyed because by doing so they have judged themselves as worthy to die, because they thought it was ok to kill their neighbor. if the world allows this it will be their judgment of themselves that they are worthy of death as well. As I have told you and Jesus showed you the first death cannot hold you but by allowing this type of activity you have separated yourself from God's law. and you will receive what you sought to be isolated and alone forever apart from and unable to participate in heaven. Ask and ye shall receive seek and ye shall find since you have deemed yourself apart from and are willing to allow others to suffer you will suffer more.

All of this and more is what is coming the first three books I have written were to help you find that place Jesus prepared for you now not after you are dead. I have started with what is going on in our world on a national basis, this is going to continue until you have decided to know the truth and either decide to learn of that place or suffer so much you have no choice. There are many more examples worldwide, but this has the scale that it could escalate to worldwide destruction very easily. I don't believe it will end the struggle just increases the suffering. It is an example of no matter how large or how small your conflict it will still be yours until you learn to stand together or fall apart. because you see this as political to divert it from you. however, since the politicians use your authority to do what they want unless you become active in talking to your neighbors about what you believe is right then you are giving them the right to order your loved ones to give their lives for what they want. I will now deal with what I also saw on a much narrower scale because as I have said I want to talk to you since you are the source of all things that you give power over yourself. I know that I have not answered the individual concern of the first death, but that is because you have not heard. Mercy is the right God gave you to decide what you are willing to live for. that means if you seek to be dead and apart from each other and the creator of all you will be. I don't know if you have ever suffered the horror of being alone that is hell, and it is what you guarantee yourself when you think you have the right to judge one another. What does that mean, if you think you can decide who will be in heaven you have not been able to see their heart or why. if they live as Jesus did, they are more like him than many people who have lived in church. How many elderly or disabled people have you checked on or assisted? How many relatives have you shut out? how many children have you intently listened to? How many people have you taken the time to get to know? I hope that most will have numerous answers to each of these, but I doubt it. we judge what we cannot even know, and instead of finding ways to be together the world teaches us to be apart, that we are unworthy of being together, I have seen what we would call the anti-Christ he is amazingly charismatic, and he will teach what you want to hear the being apart and judging is good. The media will love him because he preaches what they have sought, to divide the people for so long now. his message can sound great, like socialism it never leads to being one with God and his creation. he presents it as your will would be God not as Jesus taught the Father's will is what matters. in this way you can recognize him in spite of his charisma which makes you want to like him. Remember to divide is always less than what could have been. look for ways to share with each other not ways you are different, all have things they are gifted to do that in itself requires us to have differences. You are not to judge them but watch how they Judge themselves and then treat them accordingly or suffer from your failure to give them what they work for. if they work for separation give them separation. If you fail to do this, you invite evil into your life, and it will continue to separate you until you feel such misery that you will ask the Father and he will show you the truth as he did me. How many times have you looked at someone and decided you did not want to have anything to do with them? Why, there are people who are to be avoided, but let it be because of how they judge themselves not because of how you judge them. In other terms, people who are to be avoided generally will let you know very quickly they are to be avoided. but let it be because of what they said or did not because you thought they would be unacceptable to your friends. Do not participate in the mob mentality. all of us have probably done things that we would probably do differently if we had to do them over again. however, those feelings that arise from those are what you must forgive yourself for and go and sin no more.

In telling you what I saw you must understand that much of it was confusing to me since it sometimes seemed so contradictory until God showed me the purpose of them. just as to many who will read this, it seemed impossible to me, I thought this could not be real, but it kept on happening. I wondered if I had lost my mind. As I had said I saw what I would think were snippets of events because some seemed so disconnected but then I was shown how they all fit together and could and would happen simultaneously. for instance, there will be people who because they have heard they were unworthy their entire lives will think that their suffering is what they should have. And there are some who think because they have listened to the church for their life they will never have to suffer, and they will think because they suffer everyone else must suffer. Yet there are others who seem to go on without significant difficulty. As though nothing could or did touch them. The horrible events of wars, financial ruin and individual misery were continuing to happen, but it seemed to have no effect on them. People were arguing and blaming each other for the misery in the world and tearing their societies, churches, and social groups apart. Seeking to blame someone other than themselves for the condition of their world. The more misery drove more acts of violence to the point that the fear of being killed drove people to further disengage with the society around them, even if this did not truly relieve them. There were many who blamed it and asked the church why they did not warn them of the misery. Some concluded that God doesn't really exist. They never took the time or thought about the reality of how their willingness to accept the judgment of others affected their judgment of themselves. Nor did they think about what God's will was for them and how he arranged all of the forces so we would have to judge ourselves and by our own judgment we receive what is next. we wanted God to submit to our will not to submit to his will. That giving us the results of what our will produced we could be so miserable to ourselves and each other. It is the fact that I saw such misery and at the same time people who seemed to be ok that made me unsure about what I was seeing. I thought if there had been a nuclear war the planet would be decimated yet there seemed to be some relatively unaffected. At the same time, there was much of the world that was struggling. then it was made clear to me that those who were struggling were putting their faith in men and what they taught, and others were not

23

allowing others to dictate to them what they were permitted to have. These people took what they had and tried to increase the value of it. They knew that value was only possible for those who understood that in order to share what was value they had to share it with others who were capable of appreciating value. giving to someone who cannot or does not share the same value reduces the value to nothing. The people who were suffering were people who were consumed with judgment. They did not understand that to judge means you remove the possibility of increasing value because in order to judge you have to choose less than what was possible. just as in their own feelings when they judge to automatically eliminate the ability to share with all involved. this will destroy every social structure eventually just as socialism cannot exist with freedom because it requires you to break God's law by taking from someone to overcome the problems they have created for themselves, as though it were the human thing to do. because they do not understand that God wants and created this time and place or portion for us to decide whether we would increase it by giving help to each other not by being forced to by others. that when given freedom the fear of loss is removed because each has the ability to raise their own standard as well as helping others to raise their value because that is how you increase the value for all. Without freedom all you have left is fear. You can say there is no God but if you do not do what God's law says you will fail and lose no matter what others say. I saw people who after searching themselves and the world understand that your fear in this world eventually comes down to the fear of death. Since Jesus showed you that there is indeed a way to live as a man and know that the first death has no hold over you, with that loss of fear they stand up without fear of others. they know that the first death is not the problem the second death is chosen by you because you judged yourself willing to be apart from God and his children because you cannot control them. Therefore, if you do not judge you do not throw away all of the possibilities to raise the value or joy of living. How does this work? know that the father wants more for you and he gives you the opportunity to either raise the value or joy of living or throw it away. the same thing that you say, or most people say they want for themselves. more joy in life that heaven itself is full of people who live to increase the Joy and value of life knowing

24

that everyone else in heaven feels the same drive. Unfortunately, most people do not understand that they have the ability to do either and that this place exists so that they will receive what they seek. consequently, when they seek things that will set them apart, they will be apart forever. All of this is what the messiah showed you and proved to you by his resurrection.

It was all these things that I saw that made me ask why are you showing me all this? He said to tell them what you see. I said that they won't listen to me, perhaps you should find a famous person, a religious leader or a political world leader. He again said tell them what you see. I was overcome with awe and decided that even though there were things I did not immediately understand I would do as I was told. As it became complete and here again, I was still consumed with awe and it took me so long to think if it were a dream it would go away, instead it stayed with me even though I could not remember what I did the day before I remembered every second of this even years later. It was constantly with me, although I was still reluctant to do as I was told I began to look for ways to do what I was told. the clarification to me was continuing so I could not do anything what I was told. Thankfully I got to the point that I really understood that the truth of the resurrection was for us to know not to fear the first death because this is only a portion of what life is. Besides it will not change the fact that no one gets out of this alive. death is part of this portion as well because it is for us to judge ourselves for what comes next.

Chapter 4

HAVE TOLD YOU WHAT I SAW but this is how I was shown to interpret it. I want you to consider it for yourself because if it is to serve you well you have to prove to yourself the validity of what you have seen. My understanding is because of the ongoing proof that what I have seen is true every time. I hope as you read it you saw it as well, but I can only tell you what I saw. That is what I was told to do. I have told you of my trepidations of actually telling people because to people they think I am trying to separate myself from them or to somehow say I am more special or holier than them, but I am in fact trying to show we should not seek to be apart from but

together as one family with the same father for all. As I considered all of this, I went to the source I know as the messiah Jesus and what he himself said to those who would come after and at his time. I know that if something is true it does not change but sometimes the context, we hear it in can make it appear to be different. If you consider what he said and then did to prove his point you cannot help but understand that he is the one that was foretold and just as pertinent today. I am committed to doing as he said and not trying to change his words to say what I want them to. I have said this is a portion we were given to judge ourselves in what we are and what we give the power to give us feelings. Since it is a portion, it requires a starting point and an ending point which is why no one can avoid the first death. Even the messiah was required to die to prove what he said was the truth. He said he is the way be as he is pick up your cross and follow me. I know people think that the rapture is going to let them avoid this but all it means is your focus will be on the will of the Father not your own will, just as Jesus' focus was. The part of two people walking, and one is gone refers to the other, not allowing them to formulate what they should think or feel. That is the kingdom God gave each of us. How many people do you talk with that do not listen or care what you say? Because their focus is different than yours. If you think about what Jesus said after his resurrection when he told Thomas to put his hand on his side, he was pointing out that while I am sure it was unpleasant pain was not overwhelming.

Again, about focusing and seeking to understand the father's will.

Some of the things I saw were about the foundation of the life each will feel. For instance, we all think of anger as a basic emotion of life. Part of that is because we are taught that it can be good. Even many of our churches teach what they call righteous anger. There is no such thing because anger requires judgment and judgment always involves the loss of value. They point to Jesus overturning the money changers' tables in the temple. First, he did not attack any individual, he was expressing his sorrow at what the church had supported and how they had diminished the value of what they taught. Second, they point to Sodom and Gomorrah, assuming that God reacted out of Anger, when in fact he reacted to protect his children. He gave them what they valued, which was harm to others. As a father, I am sure it was not anger but sorrow that they received what he did not want for them. Consider for yourself what anger does in your life and what you feel as a result of it. Jesus said judge not lest you be judged, anger requires judgment. You think because it is not what you value you must destroy it. When in fact all you are doing is removing another way to make things all they could be. Just as Jesus did with the money changers tables I call on the Churches to cease teaching any kind of anger as a suitable means of response. I always wondered as a child why religious people always seemed so angry, it is because they think it is the way they should respond to something other than what they know. It in itself is a manifestation of fear, if you call yourself a Christian you are supposed to act as he taught you to. Like him, you should never react in anger. Even what we call judgment day will not be God or Jesus reacting in anger only giving you what you sought and valued if it is to be apart from you will

27

be. Again, judge not because any time you judge you will feel bad or worse than you should have. Instead observe how everything judges itself and respond accordingly not because of your value but because of how they demonstrated their value, that will lead to true justice. In order for heaven to exist here you must not judge. Your feelings are too precious to waste them on things you cannot change. What you do with each circumstance will lead to more joy in living or bad feelings for yourself. I saw wars and suffering because people thought they had the right to judge others, it is what social structures are built on because it requires the willingness of others to submit to the will of others rather than stand for what is right. The concept of being better than, or worth more than others remove the value they could have had. However, do unto others as you would have them do unto you. If you approach another in anger that is the response you will automatically receive. You set the trend for that interaction. Because you are not better then it will cause loss always. We are all children of the father even though each individual may not know or refer to him by the same name. Just as God told Moses you cannot name me because no name can contain me, I am that I am. We kill each other over a name because when we think we can name him then we can define what he wants rather than allowing each to judge themselves. We go even further than that by trying to mitigate the consequences of their actions. Then wonder why there is no courtesy or manners anymore. It is what we teach, and the primary reason that socialism will always lead to the loss of freedom and value. That is the reason it was and is the abomination that causes desolation. I cannot maintain true value let alone increase the value for those who submit to it. That is not political, that is a fact, not an opinion. For centuries it has been known and tried and it destroys whatever people submit to it in fairly short order. So, you see that your feelings establish your value and since no one can order your feelings to change if you do not allow them to, your world is your individual kingdom. That is dominion. All of this I saw and was taught because I have grown up in a world that says they want heaven yet does not allow the groundwork for heaven to exist even though they were told all these thousands of years ago and shown the truth of them throughout history.

I saw wars and rumors of wars throughout the world. I saw people carrying on their lives without regard to the losses that occurred daily. I saw people who were content to allow others to dictate to them both their worth and their relationship with the Father of All. I cried at the loss of so much that we had been given freely because we refuse to allow others to share at their own pace and value. Which made them not want to share at all because when forced it loses its true value. The concept of giving gladly becomes nonexistent. Because of the greed of those we are seeking to help. I saw others who really tried to live their lives as they had been told was good only to find out that in truth what they believed would set them free made them a prisoner of the will of others. At the same time, there were some whose faith delivered them to a place of peace internally and did not suffer from the fear of the first death, and also lived their life as they were shown by Jesus without fear of the first death and fear of the church or social groups or men.

These were the children that because of their faith truly did pick up their cross and follow me. You cannot change the world for others only show them there is a better world they could have and hope they will seek it for themselves. Thinking someone else should die for them removes the consequences of what they do in their hearts and minds. Jesus did not die for them he lived so they would see if they lived as he showed them, they need not fear the first death. I ask you now are you angry? Do you feel alone? Have you ever considered what heaven would be like? Are you afraid of dying? Do you believe what Jesus told you and showed you through his resurrection? In order to find that place he prepared for you, you have to know these things not just think about them or hope they exist. I know how hard that is and even when you ask the father, he shows you all of this and more because you still have your own will, and until you make it completely subservient to God's will you will have doubts. I know you look at the prophets and even Jesus to find their humanity and wonder can this makes you superhuman but consider this when Jesus was on the cross even then he asked the Father once, why have you forsaken me? It shows he was the son of man, but his willingness to submit to the father's will no matter what shows that he was also the son of God. What you believe will determine how much suffering you will experience. This is how he showed we are not apart from the Father but one with the Father if we choose his will.

As I said I saw many people suffering, yet some dealt with it seemingly effortlessly As a man I thought of war naturally perhaps nuclear, but there was not as much destruction as I would expect. Then it became clear to me there was a greater risk we do not even pay attention to, but it is as dangerous and within keeping what the bible says will happen because it deals with believing in lies as though they were truths, and yet people develop their lives around this lie. If the economies of the world collapsed there would be much the same effect on the people. To understand let me point out that money was mans approximation of what your feelings are worth. There was a time when in order to provide support for this approximation we used a rare commodity such as Gold to back up the value. If the economy collapses gold will not feed you or clothe you, it won't shelter you. It is simply because it was pretty looked good and was relatively rare. But it seemed to emote feelings in a lot of people, so it seemed to possess value. Since true value is your feelings and no one but you can truly decide their value. No one can make you feel anything but pain if you do not allow them. Consequently, even though we want to make the value of gold true it is based like your money on consumer confidence therefore in actual true value it is a lie. It cannot buy your life or true love or any feeling you refuse to allow it to. so you see what it said is true believing lies as though they were truth, and even worse allowing it to determine your life. There are those who that know while money is nice as far as helping your life to be more comfortable, it must never be promoted to the level that it is life itself. That is why I have written to tell you and show you that if you base your relationship with the fatherwho loves you and wants greater things for you, and you choose to accept that he knows what he is doing and that even death is not a challenge. You begin to make the most of what you have and find there are many things you spent so much time seeking that you did not need to make your life greater.

In fact, you find that you learn to enjoy other things more than you did before because you don't take them for granted. This does not mean you will not have any obstacles, only that you will help each other to overcome the real obstacles you face. This is what will be and the reason I started with the books is to help you find the place of absolute certainty that Jesus showed you, is in you. It is this kind of understanding and certainty that will take away the fear.

With this certainty and the understanding that you are unique and especially loved by our father and knowing he loves each other this way, you will stop judging each other. True judgment then can occur and those who sought the Abomination that is socialism will receive what it ultimately leads to that is desolation. You see between the fact that currency is not backed by true value and the fact that socialism requires victims to steal from it because it encourages the failure to produce more, it will destroy those nations that adopt it as it has done throughout history. The concept of socialism is again a lie and in order to exist it has to violate God's law and that is why it cannot support freedom or Concepts of God, outside the idea that your social group is your God. When the lies that they based their social structure collapses the society also collapses so if you depend on others, you will collapse as well. And yet those who put their faith in the truth that is based on their own relationship with what is within them will find ways to help others who also seek to serve and make things greater for those who seek to overcome and work at it as well as believe and know that it is not only possible but destined to happen. What this means is that those who are incapable of existing in heaven will support the things that will destroy them. And in Amazingly short order because of the magnitude of people wanting to take from others, they will destroy themselves. As this happens more and more people will see the error of their existence as they know it and seek to change. This change in the center of the individual will result in the end of Days as you know them. It is not the end of time, just the new beginning that accompanies heaven on earth. As I hope you can see what I saw was horrific and it made me unable to not do what I was told, to tell them what you see. I have tried not to see them since that time, but they are what will be. I hope that they provide the impetus for you to reflect and find your peace.

It is there but it requires you to choose it and it is not subject to what others think and do. Let us talk about how heaven comes to be. it requires you to teach the individual relationship with God, not the churches, they are there to celebrate with others the love you individually have for the Father of all. For instance, you must train your children and relatives there are legal orders and illegal orders. To fire into a crowd with a gun is an illegal order. As long as that crowd is not physically threatening individuals. Because if you understand and are committed to changing the world you must not use violence, because it will only lead to more violence. If you are in a crowd and someone near you is violent either distance yourself from him or join together disarm him and turn him in. If you do not the chances of the police or army firing into the crowd increase, and you may die anyway. In order for this change to happen without violence, if someone is speaking of dividing the people, stand up and turn your back on them. If they speak of someone as if they are not as worthy of life as you stand up and turn your back on them.

Do not vote for them to provide political power for them. If you do you are just as guilty as them, ask the people of Sodom and Gomorrah how that worked out for them. The power they have over you is what you gave them, if they make murderers of your children, you allowed it. This applies all the time to the news media if they are trying to incite you against another or are pushing you to vote to give away your freedom, they are not trying to serve your good. If the police or army does fire into a group of people with their backs to them who do not threaten them, they need to face murder charges. If a judge does not hold them accountable hold the judge or the politicians accountable for the death again do not vote for either. It will take the whole population not just the immediate area to overcome the evil you have allowed to form. Doing this without violence will change because it removes the self-defense claim, and it really exposes who they are. You wonder why things have gotten to this point because you would not stand up for your freedom. Obviously, as the world becomes less capable of feeding and clothing the people will flee to go to places, they think are more plentiful instead of staying and making their country more productive and fruit full. Generally, what occurs is that those who seek more do not use what they have and expect it to be free to them. This will only make the country they flee to like the country they left. Foreign aid must be made to go to the people it was intended to not to companies or politicians who pocket it or spend it on what they want, if it does not it should be stopped. That way they will be forced to come to the conclusion of standing up for themselves. Everybody wants heaven to be free so they don't have to be accountable for it, but, to exist everyone in it must live in it like they want to be there and help each other to remain there. So many want God to force them and others to be there but that would not be heaven because mercy requires that you choose your values. That is how you will receive, determined by your choice. I know it sounds incredible to many now but between wars and economic collapses, you will be forced to make your choice not because that is what God wants for you but because you allowed it to come to this. In order for you to get to the place that Jesus showed you there has to be a certainty beyond any doubt which requires a love of the Father's will to take away the fear.

People consider that the resurrection was just as impossible by our understanding, but not only did it happen, but he told them ahead of time it would. How is your faith? I ask that now but there will come a time when that question determines what comes next for you. How much suffering will it take for you to say enough? Like so many you want someone else to do it for you, but if they do, they will be the ones in heaven, not you. Not because the father wants that but because you chose that. Without your free choice to be in heaven, it will not exist for you. And without your willingness to live like heaven, you need to be accountable to yourself and God. It is just a lie when it says give gladly, not because you are made to but because you want to make your world a better place.

At the same time, the world is going through the process of making you choose. Considering the war in Ukraine both countries are exceeding the financial means to carry on. They borrow from others China the US etc. yet China the US and Russia owe tremendous amounts they don't dare call in their loans because their financial system is not capable of providing the value. It is after all based on people's confidence and that confidence comes from their ability to destroy whoever tries to collect. In order for this to continue they have to come to a consensus that will not destroy each other. War will require more now not allowing time to buffer the shock of the amounts to the people and eventually, someone will have to call in their debts in order to continue being a viable economy even if it is built on make-believe. Someone will call in their debt which may force another war in order to distract from financial ruin or to demonstrate that you can't get money from someone who is more dangerous than you. Any or all of these scenarios could happen at any time wars just escalate the chances. Look around the world today how many nations with how many people are unable to raise the quality of life for their people or the majority of their people? Now suppose that God showed them they have no choice because they are going to die, so why do they waste the time they have with fear? When if you really trusted the Father as Jesus did and refused to support the evil or politicians and news media that support the evil. Now you may understand why you have been taught all of your life that you are not good enough and that it is someone else who can make you good enough only that someone else said just the opposite. He said to forgive others and yourself you are the children of the father. What if the world really believes him and does not allow the division and judgment of each other but instead holds the individuals accountable for how they judged themselves by what they said and did? Without fear this is what will happen, the media and the politicians as well as the financial institutions no if any of the fantasies that they rule by are challenged will fail. I know this sounds so impossible but there are so many reasons why this is going to happen, I have seen it and was told to tell you what I saw. Perhaps this is seemingly too scary for you so I will begin to show you the basics that I saw that make this not only possible but probably no matter how you perceive life.

In the beginning, was God in the form of all energy that is self-contained and diverse? He could do and be anywhere all the time because all that was fashioned by him. The energy was in concert and working to increase always. As they worked with the different types of energy they created form, or should I say he created form. It was different than the forms we see now because the need for matter did not exist yet. This was heaven and as I said it was different than what we know today because the forms were not confined by time or space. But there were forms one of them was the Tree of Knowledge of Good and Evil. The purpose of that tree was to warn the people that there are things that must exist to increase all. As a result, it is said that Lucifer convinced Adam and Eve that eating the fruit of this tree would make them like God himself which is why he said do not eat of this tree. In reality, the tree was there because the knowledge is that good always leads to more and that evil divides and is always less than what could have been, the reason you were not supposed to eat of it was that once you start dividing you can divide everything, and you lose sight of the fact that it requires everything to make up your world, even heaven. But since they ate the fruit, they released the division therefore a new creation had to occur to contain it again. This became the portion we would be given which, because it was only supposed to be a portion required the ability to move back to a place not linked to time and space. So, our spiritual form had to know a physical form that could be discarded as we return to our spiritual energy state because God is All energies, we were a part of him, and now he had given us our physical form he gave that physical form the energy of life which is him. All of this Jesus told you when he said in the beginning I was in my father, he is in me and we are one that is because Jesus never sought his own will only the fathers. If you look at the reaction of Adam and Eve, they were ashamed because, for the first time, they were apart from everything around them and knew this was not good, they tried to hide from the Father.

That is the first example of how evil works it divides it separates it is always less than what should have been. It is the knowledge of good and evil. If you understand this, you can always recognize evil in its varied forms. This is the story of knowing and recognizing good and evil. Sin is different and I will expose that shortly. So many of our words have lost their meaning because we have chosen to believe things that are close to but not the same as what the word was supposed to mean again you could say a communication problem, but I think it is the partial truth that Lucifer told them. Since they get to choose, they can make themselves seem like gods in this place. Poor communication can be used to mask improper intent. Because of all of these things the new creation, a physical creation, was tied to time and space because it had to be a portion which meant a starting and ending place which, the individual would be accountable for themselves. So, we have Eden which became Earth in the transformation from energy or spiritual to physical. The primary purpose of all of this is the nature of God himself, he always increases or, gets greater in every form. Since that is his nature, this creation would reflect that which is how what we call nature functions as a means to keep this creation performing the purpose it was created for. I will provide further examples of this later in my prove it to yourself section. This and much more is what I saw, so I hope you can see why I was amazed and frankly afraid of being selected to tell them what I saw. We have not understood from the beginning the purpose of creation so how could we understand its function of it? We thought it was about us but it is about the nature of our father who we are part of and supposed to be one with. Perhaps now you can understand our instinct to try to have everything apart from and not part of us because it requires you to know the purpose of or the will of our Father. This brings me to something else I saw and was reluctant to talk about that is what we call the war in heaven. When Lucifer and some other angels were ejected from Heaven. This is hard because as the spirit or energy forms that angels are it is hard to imagine a physical barrier that could prohibit them from anywhere.

But in keeping with all the Father's will is above all and there were some angels that did not like the idea that men could be apart from and free to choose the Father's will that could make them eligible to create heaven in this creation because even as energy forms they were required to be part of what his will was and not apart from his will which to them meant that they didn't have the freedom that men would be given. But as energy forms, they must go where the source puts them, so they were ejected and that makes them less than what they were accustomed to being so there was resentment of man. This is apparent in the story of Jesus and the Legion. It should be noted that Jesus did not have to use force to cause the removal of the legion but that as a being of energy, he cannot stand against the source of all energy. So, there are forms that are out there that you really should avoid, and if they seek division do not invite them in. You see the only way to be in heaven is to seek the Father's will which is always to get greater. And it is your ability to increase the joy and value of being that will allow you to exist in heaven. Any type of judgment automatically results in less than which removes you from heaven in all forms. I hope that you will see that hell is being apart from the father and all that is his, which is why loneliness can be hell on earth.

As I saw all of these things, I was being educated to understand what they meant and why it was important to tell them what you see, at the same time because I am besides what I was in spirit there is a son of man the fear of death still had a considerable amount of sway in my thought process. While I was there, I still knew I was me and that at some point doing what I was being told to tell them would immediately cause them to deny and strike out because it really takes away all of the power source that other people give them. The service to the Father and making all greater is so foreign to them since they feel apart from yet able to sway others to accomplish what they want. The concept that what they want may be opposite what the Father's will is may cause them to strike out. So, while I did not feel I could really question God I registered my concerns and hoped it would release me from this task. It was only after seven years did, I understood enough to know I was going to die no matter what, I didn't want to be the one who did not do the father's will. That understanding and the loss of the fear of death is what finally allowed me to write the first books, even then I was cautious about what I said because this is so impossible to imagine, let alone live through. I know since I experienced all this and still it took seven years to write it, I see why it might be difficult to accept. The consoling factor for me is that the sight is still with me, and the understanding is so obvious that anyone who thinks about these things can certainly prove them to themselves. That and knowing that everything must happen in his time comforts me because I know his will be done in his time it is not my place to decide when that time is for anyone else. In this book, I am doing what I was told to do and telling you what I saw.

As I have said I have continued to see how all of this is not only pertinent but required if you seek to understand this creation enough to actually be able to exist here once it becomes heaven here. The world of men evolved seeking what they considered power. The result was that they arrived at the concept of might makes right. Again, power to them required separation and judgment. The concept of true power is making life greater for all without judgment is so foreign to them that they cannot see it is the only way to lasting peace. Just as accepting the will of the father and finding ways to accomplish that. Same peace within yourself. Throughout history, men have claimed divine right to rule over other men. Tracing or trying to show they have descended from someone who has been recognized as someone in God's favor. Even though they do not show the aspects of divine guidance, mercy, wisdom, or justice. Still, they were able to convince their backers to give them their power be it through financial or special rewards. As a consequence, many nations and people have suffered. Men have sought to put themselves in positions of authority generally to gather riches. When they waiver from that traditional role they are vilified and attacked. Because people seek to be apart from so they can judge one another there is an outline they consider acceptable and unfortunately, it usually includes taking from the people with promises to do for the people and then not doing it or accusing others of permitting you to do what you said. This has been true in many of men's forms of government, democracies included, but kingships, and emperors, it is unfortunately after they assume power and remove freedoms that it finally causes the revolution for change. Each of them thought they were powerful enough to dictate what they wanted. The prominent people who benefit from their removal of freedom find ways to try and sway the population to allow their mishandling of people to continue, the fact that men have traditionally tried to hide the true nature of the meaning and knowledge of good and evil is so that if they can mask what they do long enough the people won't catch on till their freedoms are gone. Without freedom the only outcome that is inevitable is revolution. That is what has happened repeatedly throughout history. It continues today. Nations are taught they are better than or worth more than others and eventually the belief in what you have been told is so strong you are willing to give the lives of your family to prove it and put other people down. Or that someone has more than you have so you must take it is another ruse used to destroy families. The churches teach separation and judgment to the point of militarizing their followers which involves judgment they order the killing of other people over a name they give God who is beyond the ability of any name to contain. What they describe as god is what they demand that others be driven by to the point of the elimination of those who disagree. Then they call themselves Christian even though Jesus never called for any of it. They refer to Jesus as God himself, yet they do not even listen to what he told them to do, and not to do. For the same reason God told Moses no name can contain me because you cannot define me anything you name you think you can define but you cannot define me, I am that I am. If from the foundation of these churches, the cannot be in keeping with their own foundation and lineage why do you not question them, even more important if you are supposed to be like Christ why do you not see through his eyes? Why do you follow so many teachings that are directly opposite of what he himself said? Everything in all my books relates directly to what he said. If you are of another religion look at its lineage if it goes back to the father of all there is nothing in these books that is contrary until you seek to name God. I have said repeatedly in each book I am not here to tell you what you must believe I merely point out how the truth is in the things that have been said and challenge you to consider them for yourself. What is different is that like my vision I know God the Father wants to hear from you and bless you if you are willing to help yourself with true understanding, ask him I will answer what people ask me he will answer for himself if you have enough faith to ask him. Again, what I saw was coming here. The suffering of so many is because they will not understand evil until they have suffered enough to be unable to take anymore. Because so much of it is caused by failing economies that were based on what really doesn't exist, yet they have defined themselves by money, another false God. Some will reach the point of total despair because of the loss of so much that they valued but find out what was really of value they took for granted when they had it. Others will mourn the loss of their social status and recognition as an important person. There will be those who seek the Father's will and try to see the world through Christ's eyes they will be able to find the place he told you about so you will not need to fear. It will be between the collapse of economies which will lead to lawlessness throughout the world until so many reach that point of no fear. Then they will hear the rest which is that the violence they see around them is not the answer. It will only lead to more. They have taught their children the frustrations we give ourselves by doing what we should not. Not by man's law but by God. Coupled with allowing things to judge themselves they will be able to stand against the tyranny of mob rule. Not by fighting but by turning their back.

Refusing to give support to the leaders the media or anyone who seeks to divide. They will without fear expose those among them that seek violence. The police and the army will not follow illegal orders and fire into the civilians with their backs turned any officer or person who does should be shot because he is willing to kill someone's family therefore, he has judged himself worthy to die. Finally, all of those who stand up and turn their backs on the leaders or media that seek to promote division and conflict will remember and they will vote against those people who have judged themselves by division which is evil. The election officials will not allow the falsification of elections because they will be discovered and by doing that, they deserve the punishment they were willing to give their countrymen. People will not judge but you will be held accountable for how you judged yourself by what you did. This will help others to have faith in God that allows them to join others and soon whoever is addressing the people be it politicians or media will have to begin to seek to bring together not separate which will cause the people to stand up and turn their backs on them. Obviously, this is not easy but the world as you are allowing it to be by allowing those things that will not and cannot serve the good of all to be the ruling factors in your social groups your church your schools even your houses will continue to divide that is what evil does and will always do. Until you have the faith that Jesus had even to not fear death but to fear failing the Father you will not have the strength it takes to end this cycle and you and your children will suffer as victims of it. It is time if you understand these things talk to each other draw strength from each other it is not apart it is together in such a way as to not violate the law of God that will require more strength than perhaps you think you have. But just as impossible as what I saw seemed to me at the time God makes the impossible fact, what will happen is that very quickly your neighbors will become inspired and even the military itself will return to the people the control of their country. The media that have been living on the political largess of those who finance the political system will see very quickly they have no popular support because they failed their primary function which was just to report the news not make the news. Do not call for justice unless you are willing to be held accountable for what you have done.

You can decide for yourself what is to be for you. What I have seen is the end of days as you know them. If you hear the words Jesus told you again and you still do not seek our Father you will destroy yourselves through your nuclear weapons and there will be survivors and they will hear and understand. Time is something for you to worry about, our spirit is not tied to it.

Consequently, what I have seen will happen and heaven will be restored without division those who seek to be apart will be. Not because I want it or the father wants that but in their portion they have judged themselves as wanting to be apart. Heaven will be made whole will you be in it?

Chapter 5

THIS IS WHAT I AM SAYING, I am that I am I do not exist because you make me, You exist because I made you and love you and want to spend eternity raising the Joy and value because that is what I am. That is the purpose of this portion that you receive now, it is so you can judge yourself and decide how much eternity you will share. I gave you the freedom to judge yourself not each other, because only you and me can truly know why you have chosen to feel about anything.

Therefore, if you choose to be apart you will be apart. Ask and you shall receive seek and you shall find. It is all because of the individual, not society or the social group. I am once more reaching out to you so that you will know and stop destroying yourselves and each other. It is each of you that I have made and love, it is your decision to love or to die and be apart from. It is for each of you to decide not for your church or your society or whatever false Gods you have elected for yourself. They do not love you and want to separate you from all. Since the beginning, which is me, I have given you many things to learn to love each other and me but you have continually separated all of them, in your lust to control. Before time itself which I created so you could have this portion. I am when the planet or room you call home was just a rock with single-cell life that multiplied enough so that its product could create the atmosphere you need to live I am. The many years that it took to develop all of this so you would have the chance to choose to live, for me was an instant. Still, you choose things to be apart from and do not understand there is a purpose for all, so no matter why you don't like it, it is therefore my purpose which is to always get greater. You think the loss of you would not allow that if you seeking to be apart from what you do not want to be part of. It is only in your choice to love and seek to be together that makes the increase I am. Instead, you seek the use of force to make you do my will, but my will has always been that you would always choose to want to increase the joy of life for all because I love All. Gain this is for each and every individual that I am using this means to talk to you. Not what others think or say but what each individual heart is for. You are so concerned about life as you know it that you feel you can judge and persecute others. You do not seek to live you seek to judge, and because of that, you allow others to tell you what you are right to judge. This had to be part of the Plan as well. This thinking was apparent and used when I gave you the messiah, you say he came to die for you. In truth, he came to live for me. In that way, you can know what you have been told is true. Let us consider the history of man and compare it to the intent or purpose of creation.

As we look back, we see many instances of man's interaction with God. Generally, any tie there was interaction with any heavenly messenger or individual there was a tendency to make them Godlike however, they would immediately tell you not to do that. This is because it is not the individual but the relationship of all to God that you will be judged by. When you judge things, you think you can define or limit them. God is greater than you can imagine.

This is what he told Moses when he gave him the Law which was immediately used to separate and judge the people instead of being used to provide a pattern of living for the individual, it became a tool to be used to force compliance to someone else's interpretation of what it said. It was for the individual so as a consequence the socialization of it reduced the true purpose of it. Then we were told of a coming messiah Again the socialization of it became used as a way to divide and control the people. Again using it as an excuse to use force, even without understanding that it is for all the children not just the social group. Then we see when he came it was in a manner no one expected or could have predicted. He also did not do what they wanted him to do use force to remove those they did not want. Because he did not live for them or their social group but lived instead in pursuit of the father's will, they decided he must die. Which had also been foretold. Then they used this death to reinforce what they believed which is death. They had to say he died for you, even though the fact of the matter was he lived for the father. It was done this way so you could understand the things he told you about. The first death and the second death. Even though he died the first death he lived to prove to you what he told you was true, which is to live for the father and to love all of the children and not judge. They have changed it into the most vicious form of judgment throughout the generations. You see division is always less than it could or should have been. That is the nature of evil and the knowledge men think they control but it was and always has been the individual, not the social right to control. There were many other interactions usually warned or told that were going to happen. I will allude to many of them throughout this narrative. Mostly in defense of what I saw and was given to show you. Many of them will be defined by what Jesus himself told you was going to happen. To his disciples, Jesus asked, who do men say I am? Then who do you say I am? All of this so that they would understand what they were receiving was extraordinary. Then he went on to tell them what was coming and that he was to become a sword, not the peace men said they were seeking, again because of social interaction and groups not because of what he said or taught. He described wars and the breakup of families because people would refuse to live as he showed them, they could. But men say you are not good enough and no one is worthy, Yet Jesus showed them in his life they could live as he did. He lived as the father wanted, and so can you. He sought the Father's will above his own, so can you. He had doubts and concerns about the cost of doing that just as you do. To demonstrate that when he was on the cross, he asked Father, why have you abandoned me? Then he said it is finished thy will be done.

You see you can have doubts and still do the father's will. So much for not being worthy enough, you are a child of God if you live as Jesus did try to live as Jesus did and follow the law of the individual as it was given through Moses, you may never be good enough in the eyes of men but you are always loved and enough to your father. Do not die for men, which is what society believes you must want, because that gives men power, instead do as Jesus did and live for our Father God. He said that in the end many will come to him saying lord, lord. And he will say to them why do you call me lord but do not do as I said? I don't know you. Do you now live for the father as he did? Or do you follow the church of men who killed him? You say you are a Christian, but do you do what he said? Do you think you have the authority to judge others? If you do, then you are part of the church of men that killed him. Do you put the father's will which is for all of his children above your will which would destroy those different than you? Do you make Jesus apart from and completely empowered the same as the Father? Or do you understand that even now it is the father's will he serves? Do you understand that Jesus said I and my father are one because it is the Father's will that must be done? He could not put his own will above the father's. Now you can see why every heavenly visitor and messenger told you not to worship them, it is for the father only. If you accept the will of the church of men, you have made this social creation of men your God and you are not doing what Jesus said.

Let us consider other interactions and some of their results. I am going to talk about Sodom and Gomorrah, I know there are so many unanswered questions, but I am going to talk about things we know about it. I will also give a couple of hypothetical questions I hope you will consider from the standpoint of so much unknown. I think it is important because history has a way of repeating itself. There is so much unknown about past civilizations without any solid facts to go on. But I think there is much more than we are truly aware of, and it would still be in keeping with what we know and the reasons for creation. The overall goal of creation is for us to learn what true good is and how it comes about. Unfortunately, many want to ignore a large portion of what is rather than deal with it and learn from it. That would require the individual to think for themselves which our society frowns upon because it limits their control of the individual, and it is not till they can put their spin on it so it enforces their narrative that they finally agree to address it. This is true on a cultural, social, and religious basis.

45

Again, what does someone else think? The actual causes can be so different. What we think we know it from scriptural writings is that the towns had been so corrupt that visitors were immediately in danger. Be it robbery or rape, they were certainly at risk. So as our scripture tells it God sent Lot to tell the people to flee that place because he had heard so much outcry about the injustices his children were going through so he had decided to destroy those cities. This is common for God to forewarn his children. Many did not flee for whatever reason I would guess the love of the wealth they had achieved there. So, Lott and his family fled. But his wife was so enamored with the place she turned around and was turned into a pillar of salt. The city and everything were utterly destroyed. How this happened we don't know the story tells of two angels sent to carry out the destruction.

One of my hypotheticals is that heavenly Angels can be here in matter form, but they are normally in anti-matter form we know that contact between matter and anti-matter is molecularly destructive like a nuclear explosion, which may have been the reason Jesus told Mary not to touch him because he had not gone to the father yet. And yet later told Thomas to put his hand into the wound. This is one hypothetical scenario; another would be that there were cluster munitions from a previous war there that exploded at that time or God caused them to explode. All of this is in question to what our scientist today seems to indicate the area seems to exhibit signs of a nuclear type of blast. At the same time, there are ancient depictions of weapons of mass destruction being used. Makes you wonder, what I do know is that God the Father can do anything, and that will include anywhere in the universe so if his house has many rooms, they all exist for the same purpose to get greater because he is always greater. It is not my place to question only to not judge and allow all things to judge themselves because then you can share and that is how you make things greater. You see by denying what you don't know or don't like you are reducing what is instead of finding ways to share and increase the joy for all. This may be one of the earliest lessons we failed to understand. The reason it is important is that the cities never got that way without the people allowing it. As a result, they were all destroyed. This scenario is occurring today in a number of war conflicts globally. Because the people have elected and empowered corrupt men to lead there nations and have not kept God's law in their hearts they send their sons and daughters husbands and fathers to fight and die for leaders who do not really care as much about them as their wallet. Russia seeks to steal from its neighbor, the Russian people think they are superior to Ukrainians. Therefore, they can take what they want even though it is not theirs. And for fear of nuclear retaliation, the rest of the world is allowing this. In the end, what will eventually happen is that nuclear weapons will be used, small tactical weapons so that others will be afraid. If there is no great response, they will do it again. I told you how things have a habit of recurring throughout history. This is the correct response tell the people we are coming and we will establish air superiority and destroy whatever moves on the ground if you don't want to die get away from any Russian group. If you want to be Russian go to Russia.

If you stay in your neighbor's country, you die. Just Like in Sodom and Gomorrah, the devastation to those who violate God's law should be complete. And this is what should happen in every conflict where people are violating God's law. It is because they judge themselves as murderers or support murderers that they are removed. It has nothing to do with politics, it has to do with the Father's will that we do not harm one another. This may sound cruel but how many died in Sodom that were nice folks? It really toned things down in a hurry knowing it could happen. Until the evil ones who willingly violate God's law are held responsible for what they have done and the deaths of so many innocents this will continue. If you think this is harsh, wait till you hear what's coming. Because you are innocent you should not die. Everyone including Jesus himself has to die the first death he is the Messiah because he showed you it is not the second death the only one who can cause that for you is you. While there are many innocents being killed in Ukraine and other places throughout the world those who have chosen the father will have life forever. You think that means nothing to you here and now the separation is for but a short time because we are at a place in time that has been foretold to you as well. What you do with all of this is up to you. I have seen so much that I wish there was a way to show you. But I know that eventually you will see for yourself, I hope you will have time to rejoice and enjoy the gifts you have been given.

One of the gifts you have been given is your world, not your neighbors or anyone else's world only yours. In telling you this I want you to consider rapture. A state of joy and peace and a promise of more to follow. Many people take drugs trying to capture it but it inevitably avoids them. That is the state of rapture. To so many, they think because they have been taught that you will physically disappear. And yet they do not see how their voice has been nullified by men seeking what they want. As long as you feel helpless you are physically absent. You think that God should do this for you so you don't have to deal with what is. The fact is that if you refuse to interact you have raptured yourself. If you live for the fathers, will you do not have to worry about death because Jesus showed you the first death has no hold on you? You simply have to refuse to do those things he told you not to do. You must believe that the creator of all loves you and will provide for your well-being. How can that work in this world? Refuse to be swayed by political rhetoric and concentrate on how to not divide but always seek to do that which will lead to more for everyone including yourself.

Taking from others is not the answer. Do not seek violence or anything that harms another. Do not judge each other but observe how they judge themselves and hold them accountable.do not join the crowd that reacts because someone says something about another. Justice requires that we each are accountable for what we said and did. Even if you claim to be following someone else's order, it is you who violates God's law supporting them. This is true for all even if you are in the military or law enforcement, obeying an illegal order is finding yourself guilty. To be raptured does not mean that anything ceases to exist only that you cease to be used for immoral purposes. When you vote or fail to vote, if it is used to empower evil you will still be guilty. It is better to stand up and turn your back to it, so all know you do not support it. If you know you have been told that something is going to happen, and you do nothing, you will lose more than you thought. Just as in Sodom and in hopes it would stop now Ukraine it is coming if you do not get away from it you will die not because anyone else judged you but because you judged yourself worthy by not getting out. If you are Russian and have members in the military, they are in their neighbor's land killing their people tell them to surrender or come home now. If you are Ukrainian when they surrender treat them as you would want to be treated. If they are guilty of war crimes until it is proven beyond any doubt, they did treat them as innocent. Those who do not distance themselves once they are warned feel sorry for them, but they judge themselves. Just as those who fought and died trying to protect them judged themselves worthy of serving their brother and the father. All who live for the Father will live this is what Jesus showed what made him the Messiah.

I have seen all this and more, you think it is unheard of but you will find the father does not play with war the way many of your politicians do to make money by the deaths of others. The form it will take is an announcement that they are about to take action then there will be total air supremacy and then every effort including massive artillery bombardment air reconnaissance then YJR commitment of troops. At the first shots fired that area will be isolated and wiped out. There will be no mercy for those who did not give mercy. This will continue till there is no resistance left in their neighbor's country. If necessary, there will be a demilitarized zone which must remain free of everything. Any incursion should be instant death. If this happened with world sanctions the activity of this type would cease. Any country that does not support this must be considered a conspirator for the continuation of this type of activity. And should be the recipient of total sanction, and any country that would invade their neighbor would automatically be the recipient of the same treatment. Notice I did not say wait and talk about it by entering your neighbor's property you have broken God's Law. If you say your people are there tell them to sell their property, there and come home it is not an excuse to violate God's law. There would be far fewer of our children killed by the lust of immoral leaders. And greater wealth for all of the children. But you continue the political desire to take from your brother and support your false Gods of society and money, you don't care how many sons and daughters and innocents are killed. For this reason, you leaders and all of those who put you in power deserve the first death and have guaranteed themselves the second death. Because such people will not exist in heaven.

I know this sounds so harsh if you listened to the cries and sobs of those on both sides who have lost fathers and daughters and sons and family for even a fraction of the time you would say this is too lenient. how could anyone imagine this cruelty, it is the gift man has for each other it is the gift you subject yourself to when you choose the society of men as your God. The father wiped my memory from the teachings of men so I could begin to understand the lessons I was to get. the brain injury made me capable of not seeking to argue with him about the cruelty of men he showed me. Or the coming of justice which will be. you will be accountable for what you have done and said and supported if it means anything but the sincere wish for the increase to all you have judged others and by doing so you have chosen the second death. No one but you can do this and what you have sought you will receive. If you want to be apart from others, you will be alone in hell. No one will put you there other than you. If you accept the teaching of the church that you are not worthy according to them. You have judged yourself worthy of the second death. Or that all you need to do is know the name of Jesus you are free you have chosen the second death. Why do you call me lord, but do not what I say? Get away from me I don't know you.

Live as I did for the father pick up your cross and follow me nothing costs nothing. Time begins and ends in the father and since he never ends he gave it to you to decide how much you will have.

Chapter 6

WE CAN NOW TALK MORE ABOUT the next thing to come the rapture. As I have stated earlier this is as most things not as it appears or what you have been taught at least not implicitly what you have been taught. There is an order to all things. To provide some insight I ask you who is the first who was already raptured? You may have heard of him his name is Jesus. He entered the state of rapture when he was facing crucifixion. What did it deliver him from? The judgment of men. He proved this by his resection if you want to know the place, he prepared for you we call it rapture. He entered it before his death to deliver him from the suffering that men sought for him. Because for you as for him it can only be an internal choice to live for the father and have peace in knowing the father's love of you will deliver you as well. "Peace, I have, my peace I give you." Do you not think God the Father would protect his child? He was the first to be raptured and yet he lived for the father. By living for the Father, he did not break the Father's law and he called each of you to sin no more, he would not have told you that if he knew you could not do it. But the people believe in force and judgment so if it requires of them, they seek a way that is someone else's fault. You see he was restored to life perhaps differently than most but what do you think comes after the rapture? So, who then do you think will be raptured since the church teaches you that you are all unworthy? And it is impossible to have enough good works to be worthy. For the same reason how can you know let alone be the judge of who will be raptured? I have written these four books based entirely on the words spoken by Jesus to show you what he promised you. Peace is the place of rapture, it will deliver you from the judgment of men. You live your life trying to appease men instead of trying to be as he told you to be. If anyone challenges your right to judge you condemn them. Just as the church did Jesus. But just as he had peace in spite of his crucifixion you too will have peace by knowing that the judgment of other men does not affect who you are only those things you give power over yourself has power.

What about disappearing? How much does your government or your church listen to you? Would you say you are a major concern? If you are corrupt enough to represent a substantial amount of money, they might hear you and probably give you a lame excuse about why they can't do it that way. Now supposing you went and told them God was your father and one in being with you.

That is what happened two thousand years ago and is happening around you now. It sounds crazy but what he said was in the beginning I was in my father; my father is in me, and we are one.

Because he lived for his Father's will and he died because it was his Father's will that by living again for his father, the truth of all he had said was proven. And people decided if he was one with God his will would supersede the fathers which will make him God. What he actually showed them is if you live for the will of the Father even above your own you can have the rapture to have peace and in service to the Father never be afraid. That does not mean it does not come without a doubt even Jesus doubted briefly. When he said Father why have you abandoned me? But his trust and love and faith in the Father provided for him.

So how much faith love and trust do you have in God? Is it enough? Do you think so? Pick up your cross and follow me. Being one with and serving each other and the father is what will give you the rapture and heaven. How important is that? In order to have heaven here on earth each individual who will participate in heaven must live for the Father and all that is of the Father which is everything.

You will always be able to divide things and make them less than others, but in heaven no one would seek to do that they would take the parts and use them to make the whole greater because that is what does and wants us to do in that process we will find heaven on earth. You see nothing exists without the parts, but the parts are ultimately only useful to the whole. That is how and why the tree of knowledge of good and evil was and is in heaven and it was in Eden. We would say why doesn't God just do away with it since that would force everyone to do what is right in his eyes, it is not about right and wrong it is about increase and in particular the joy of increase of love. In order for that to occur you must freely accept it and share it with others who are capable of knowing it as well. Those are the people who will reap the benefit of rapture because they will wish that everyone would love enough to join.

Everything must exist in its complete form to exist at all. That is why we have so much difficulty understanding we only look at the parts. The rapture must include the faith and understanding and love of the Father it had for Jesus to receive it so it is for you as well. So many call themselves Christian yet they do not what he said. They think it gives them the right to judge each other even though they have no idea what the other feels and values or why. If all of this sounds like a mystery to you it did to them as well. Judge not lest you be judged. How will you feel when you run to him saying lord, lord? And he looks at you and says "Why do you call me lord, yet you do not what I said? Get away from me I do not know you." That is denying you before the father.

I pray that I have done a good job of trying to flesh out for you the things I saw that he told me to tell them what you see. If this book has helped you and the other three books are helping you to truly know the peace that is the rapture that will deliver you from the judgment of men, I ask please tell your family and friends and neighbors so that they will get these works and they will help them. The peace of knowing is waiting for you, please share it so many more will join in the rapture. The obstacles are many and the trials are diverse but each of you was called into being by the creator who loves you and wants you to make the right choices to spend eternity raising the Joy of living.

AFTERWORD

MANY WILL FEEL THAT I HAVE been harsh in my books towards the church. I am simply following the vision through Christ's eyes. When Satan, whose name means adversary, tempted Christ he asked to give him everything, which makes everything property and only the rights you give them. Christ said no. The churches today seek to rule the earth in Christ's name. Again, I say to you I require mercy I do not require sacrifice. It is the value of the individual that makes things merciful, NOT your judgment of them, since you cannot see their heart, only what they have done. Unfortunately, the churches seem to promote exactly what he said not to do. Judge each other. The scriptures talk about the army of Christ men interpret that to mean punishing the ones they don't approve of. In reality, they are giving them what they seek, to be apart from and property of something other than the father. If you wish to be the property of anything other than raising the joy of the life the Father gave you, you will be returned to the dust that is the property you were made from. Property has no rights other than what you give it. The father gave you the freedom to choose property but does not have that. This is why Jesus told Satan no. his will is neither self-serving nor separate from the fathers will, he lived for. He asks you to do as he showed you how to do the same. So, I ask in his eyes which are being harsh? The church was meant to be a place of celebration of the life you were given and an opportunity to join together and raise Joy by helping each other. Not mandated but freely given. Why do you call me lord but do not what I say? All of his words were to guide and help you see the world as he did.

Changing their order and meaning to make your property is what men do. So if your church says you can judge anyone else, or describes its members or seeks members as property they are not doing what Jesus called them to do. You are children of the father the only one that can make you property is you. If you allow anything this right you have chosen the second death. It is only you that can choose that for yourself. That is the gift of salvation Jesus gave to you, and what made him truly the messiah.

"This is a non-fiction account of what I experienced, every fiber of your being seems to resonate when you are in the presence of God and you can never forget that. Even when it is over you will never forget the truth"